CARAVAN OF LOVERS

A BOOK OF POEMS

PETER JAMES CRAIG

Copyright © 2018 Peter James Craig

http://creativecommons.org/licenses/by-nc-nd/3.0/

ISBN: **1-884178-98-7**
ISBN-13: **978-1884178986 (Kairos Center)**

Cover design by Jenna Jasso and Peter

Cover photo of Sahara desert sunset, Morocco by Peter

Headshot on back cover by Yannik Rohrer, *ThePerfectHeadshot.com*

Poems written between 2011 and 2017.

To visit Peter's site, go to
Petercraigcoaching.com

To connect on Facebook, go to
Facebook.com/peterjamescraig

When you find the love, you find yourself.
The secret is in the love… Everything is in the love, and everyone needs the love. If you find this, what more could you want? When you have the knowledge of love, you feel peace in your heart… But look and reach so that you find every meaning, and do not hesitate, because inside every meaning is a quality of love. If the Muslims, Jews, Christians, and the people of any other religion, knew their religion well, there would only be one religion, the religion of love, peace, and mercy.

~ Sidi, *Music of the Soul*

CONTENTS

I. SETTING OUT

All Over Again..5
Forever..6
Love Has a Face...7
Where are You?..9
A Poem for Justice..10
Spring and Forgotten Wings..11
Sun and Rain and Moon..12
Dear One..13
The Rising Sun...13
Everything Changes..14
You are So Beautiful...15
Body of What I Believe...16
Love Poem..17
Bursting Imaginations...18
First I was a Lion..19
YOLO?...20
Cast Away..21

II. LOST IN THE DARK NIGHT

Be Your Everything..25
There Is No Other Way...26
Bridge Between Body and Soul....................................28
My Sex Is..29
Poetry Is a Pushing...30

Something Inside of Me..31
Caravan of Lovers..32
If You Slowed Down Enough..33
Praying for Everyone..34
Tell Me Why..35
Turning Closer..36
Poetry and Beer..37
Set the Truth Free..38
Poets are Drunks..39
Wow..40
One Way Through..41
Love like Water...42
Kiss You on the Lips..44
Hidden Within..45
Love Me Past this Pain..46

III. DISCOVERING AN OASIS

A Secret Door...51
The Sweetness of Your Longing..................................52
Breathe into Your Body..54
So Full of Love..55
The Moon Ties Us Together..58
Falling into You..59
Calling Out..60
What a Feeling..61
A Shining Star..62
Heart Says...63
Love Knows Your Name...64
One in Everything...65
Whispering Soon..66
I Believe in Alchemy...67
Pure Poetry...68
Opening Cages...69

A Mysterious Force..70
One Village...71
I am Not for Me..73
The Garden of Lovers...74
Axis of the World...75
Share it with Everyone..76
God's Loving Imagination...77
A Golden Wind...78

IV. COMING HOME

At the Gates..81
In a Melting Pot..82
On the Sea Floor Waiting...83
Love Languages..84
Turn to Prayer...85
All the Way Down..86
Mary Oliver...87
Be Good to Me..87
My Epitaph..89
Connecting Me to You..90
All I can Remember..91
My Eyes Are Spies..92
Beauty Comes to Me...93
Fertile Crescent...94
Master of Ambiance..95
If Your Prayers Land Close..96
The Light of Everything...97
Washing Over Me...98
The Body Calls...99
Like a Tree..100
Modern Mystics..101

*Dear global human village,
I love you.*

I. SETTING OUT

All Over Again

Noisy streets
And a restless world.
I find my peace.
I find my place.

People getting lost.
People getting found.
I find myself.
I lose myself

In You,
The great starry void,
The mystery of being,

Spiraling planets and eyes,
Falling in love
All over again.

*F*orever

If you don't believe
That love
Is hunting you down
Like a wild animal,

What *do* you believe?

Who seeks you then?

Is it nothing or
A separate force?

Words are empty,

Love tracks you down
in the middle of the night

And wakes you up
Forever.

Love Has a Face

Life gives itself
To you.

When you give it back,
You're free.

Yes whatever comes to you
Is destined,
Whatever passes through your hands,
Let it go.

Open this gift by giving.
Yes, freely
To your brothers and sisters.

You know how.
Use what you have.
Life keeps asking you every day.

Don't wait, there is no perfect moment.
This is the perfect moment.

And when you give and give and give,
And don't even ask to take, keep giving.

And just when your faith might break,
Treasures beyond your wildest dreams
Suddenly appear to you.

Yes they flow to you,
Through you,

Over and over again,
Precious treasures
Wash up to your feet.

Look down, pick them up,
Rub the golden mirrors clean

And see that Love
Has a face.

Where Are You?

Are we eternal?

The realization of life
Is death.

The realization of death
Is life.

One wheel,
One turning.

Where are You
In the churning
Of tides?

A Poem for Justice

The sound of gun shots
Ringing in my ears.
The sight of blind violence
Stoking the fears
That we cannot transcend this hate.

But brothers, sisters, friends,
As a privileged white male,
I apologize to all the discriminated against,
Let's make amends.

First loving ourselves deeper.
Next dismantling the structures
That is the ignorant keeper.

Yes, the blame lies on many fronts.
And yet the solution lives on our tongues!
Uncomfortable conversations at work or at play,
We need to recognize the inequalities
And not keep them out of mind at bay...

A bigger pain is surfacing.
A bigger need is unearthing,
That we are either one village or none!
Something must be done!

Let's pick up an instrument,
Put down the gun.
Singing *"We are One!"*
"We are One!"
Dissolving prejudice one new friendship at a time.
Harmonizing our music of the soul in one rhyme.
Is this the land of the free!?
Well then let's work to equalize equal opportunity-
Dissolve racism, sexism, genderism...can't we?

Singing *"We are One!"*
"We are One!"

Spring and Forgotten Wings

The morning
Rises, the birds
Mid-song,

Something wakes up
Inside of me.

Spring and
Forgotten wings
Unfurling.

Sun and Rain and Moon

I can feel your *yes*
Coming into me.

I can feel your sweetness
Seeping into my pores.

Hollow me out,
Make me only

Sun and rain
And moon
And You.

Dear One

Dear One,

You inspired poetry
From my lips
And chest.

Watch as these words
Rise up, then regress.

Take them in,
Shake them out,

They are yours,
You pulled them out.

The Rising Sun

It's like you turned around
And I was stunned!

My heart had something to say
Newly.

And it spilled itself all over,
Crashing the mirror!

And now you're stunned,
And now we're
One,

And I can see
The rising sun
Inside of
You.

Everything Changes

Hearts are homes,
And even they
Cover the sky.

So here I am,
An effulgent soul stream
Pouring into you.

Like water and wine,
Spilling all the time,
Suddenly illuminating!

The soul breaks free!
Between You and me—
No separation!

Bliss and a kiss,
And skin is heaven,
And *to begin is everything.*

So come with me
With bewildered sighs,
Soul-steered eyes,
Bodies overflowing like honey.

The rock is broken,
The soul shines through,

The heart bows down,
Everything changes.

You Are So Beautiful

You are so beautiful.

I am speechless but our eyes
Reveal everything.

I have nothing to offer you,
So I turn inward,
Craft carefully

A nothingness
That calls you
To loving.

Body of What I Believe

I want to arrive against the body
Of what I believe.

I want to show up to a polished mirror,
Seeing clearer and clearer.

I want to rise my passions like a great wave,
Then dissolve them into the ocean,
Forever now brave.

Love Poem

When I look into your eyes,
My heart smiles.

I can feel your whole body's love
Leaping out into the world,
And I want to hold you.

You are so beautiful.

I want to swallow your curves
Like the sun eats the moon.

We speak the language of love,
Our eyes are lips.

Our transparent hearts kiss,
And I imagine us making love.

Bursting Imaginations

What is the *state of your mind?*

More importantly-
What is the *condition of your heart?*

Yes, tell me
Of your plans.

But really I want to hear about
What your heart
Longs for
Most.

Tell me,
Will you tell me, of
Your bursting
Imaginations?

First I was a Lion

First I was a lion,
Then a hunter.

Now *I'm* being hunted!
-By the lion inside of me?

Run, run!
Bang, bang!

Who falls down,
Who rises?

YOLO?

"You only live once,"
They say,
But what if you never die?

What if we keep on living
Forever?

Things people say
Pass on
Like birds on a wire,

But if you fall off,

How far down do you go
And,
Do you have wings?

Cast Away

Cast your blinders off!

Cast away even
What served you
Getting here.

See things
At last
As they truly are.

Hoist up the mast
Of your new vision.

Sail this way.

II. LOST IN THE DARK NIGHT

Be Your Everything

It took a while,
But things fell apart.

Was it me?
Was it you?

Was it life getting
In between?

This is not a war of words,
But a nothing left to say.

This is not even goodbye,
But some kind of leaving.

What are we leaving?
The patterns in our mind?
The daily grind?

I'm wishing you the best,
But something inside of me-
Still hurting.

Maybe because I couldn't be
Your everything.

There Is No Other Way

I've been a liar,
A cheater,
A fake.

Everything you hate.

I've been a rich kid gone bad,
No one feels sad
As I fall from grace.

Trying to be something I'm not,
Bright and shiny false mirror?
How can I see clearer and clearer?

~

Here I am confessing that
I could've treated you better.
I could've not pulled away
Or conditionally stayed.

But here I am,
Asking for forgiveness.
Finally it is clear that there is no other way.

My pride is a veil,
Self-pity too.

Underneath the anger
And the fear
Is a great sadness with you.

This ocean of pain rises up again,
And the waves crash down.

I'm lost at sea and in misery
Without the words *I'm sorry.*

Now look, an island!
With each sorrow,
A rising call to prayer.

With each surrender,
More land for us to care.

Maybe one day
All the seeds of loving sorrow
Will grow into fruit,
And we can feast and say

I forgive you.

Bridge Between Body and Soul

Tell me, what is love?

Tell me, what is the difference
Between sense desires

And to what your heart
Truly aspires?

I am caught on a bridge
Between body and soul.

-Two separate ports or one infinite space
Where we all have our place?

I am falling- in love? In sex? In pain?

I am drowning,
What remains?

I am led
By so many voices,
My eyes and skin and ears
Are crying out!

Love me!
Love this!
Love that!

Shall I deny
The senses' clout?

Where does lust meet
Soul longing?

My Sex Is

My sex is a weapon,
My sex is a friend.

My sex causes conflict,
My sex makes amends.

My sex breaks windows,
My sex opens doors.

My body is a vessel,
Falling to the floor.

Something more real unseen,
My sex is a bridge in-between.

Where are you
In the crossing of tides?

Poetry is a Pushing

Poetry is
A *pushing*.

It ushers sweet, sacred words
Down stretching,
Hungry isles.

What is it that we've forgotten,
Still echoing through the halls
Into our eyes?

Something Inside of Me

What is the difference between
Humans and animals?

We were endowed with a great secret
That lives on generation after generation.

A secret that we are more than
These bodies, more than this material world.

So why can't I see it?
Why can't I breathe it?
But ah, yes we can.

Closing my eyes
I breathe in deep love,
Exhaling I forgive, letting go.

Maybe I just touched something
Inside of me.

Caravan of Lovers

I know that
She's been hiding.

Beyond the walls
No one dares to climb,
They're too high to climb.

Come down from your castle wall!
Come down from those walls which behind you hide.
We're leaving tonight.

Yes, we can, and we will
Ride into a perfect sunset
On a perfect hill!

Our dreams are coming true!
Do you believe? I do!
So come with me,
This caravan can set you free.

Do you really believe?
That you can set your heart free?
Come with me, let's set out and see,

But we're leaving tonight.

If You Slowed Down Enough

I'm bottled up baby,
Don't come too close,
I might explode!

Body or mind or heart?
Wouldn't you like to know.

Which veils are falling faster?

What I most want is the heart's goodness,
Which is the mind and body's too.

But what about that primal hunger?

Even this animalistic sex and rage
Can be a sacred canopy
To tear holes in the oppressive lies
Of this world.

But ah, protect us.
Protect this temple of soft skin
Which houses a secret so amazing,

It would turn your life upside down,
If you slowed down

Enough
To see it.

Praying for Everyone

Are you praying for everyone?

Who is slipping through the cracks?
Breaking mothers' backs?

Your love only
Shown for some,

Now leaves you
In the middle
Of the night.

Tell Me Why

Tell me true,
Do you love what you do?

If you don't,
What's your next step?

And if it isn't love,
Tell me why!

Everyday people dying,
My heart burning inside!

Tell me please,
When can we meet the needs?

Of the hungry and alone?
Are we not that way sometimes?

Isolated from others
When the heart turns away.

This is my reaching you,
Even touching skin.

If you wish,
I'll let you in.

Because you and me are human,
We're of the same essence inside.

So let us heal each other,
And save the day!

Winter is turning, and your
Heart has wings!

Flying high!
Love will never die!

Turning Closer

In the face of pain,
Becoming more beautiful.

In the face of joy,
Becoming more full
Of light.

Life experiences
Offer us a mysterious mixture
To know God.

Let everything
Turn us closer.

Poetry and Beer

    I got drunk,

    I fell down.

        Ouch.

Set the Truth Free

I've been a thumb sucker,
Mother fucker,
Daddy give me money
Just this last time.

I'll grow up soon,
Just waiting for one more
Woman to swoon.

Then I'll be *there*. Where?
Driving beyond my means,
Who cares.

Feed the ego until I'm blue in the face,
Driving like this, I can't take this race!
Too fast! Someone's going to crash!
... It's going to be me.

Forgive this enemy… Inside of me!
Who can catch him?
Who can detach him?
Maybe I need to set the truth free.

Poets Are Drunks

Poets are drunks, their words are stumbling
Out onto the streets to greet you.
Smell their breath as their wild eyes compel you.
Suddenly you start to sway and you're intoxicated!
Elated to be sharing some newfound meaning.

Come inside this tavern, we are singing through the night,
And finally you can understand why it took so long
To catch this flight. Our pain is an empty glass, but Who is refilling?
We can say cheers to the lost years, now that we've made it here.

Yes, suddenly our wounds are healed by overflowing cups,
Swinging round the room, glistening light into waves of drops
Of dreams kissing tenderly all that we've lost in our lives' scenes.
New themes emerging like a phoenix's sight!
And yes, we ride tonight!

The only life raft here is the Name of the sound of your love,
Echoing sweetly from ear to ear until we hit the floor by the door.

Waking up on the street,
We are laughing at our follies,

Giving away everything
For another sip
Of truth.

Wow

I got lazy.
I got weak.
Stopped helping others,
Was stuck staring at my feet.

Self-pity glares at the mirror,
Seeing no clearer.
Got to get out of here!

I ran to my passions,
Ran to my friends.

I ran to good food,
And what makes my heart
Feel good.

Weeks later looking down at my hands,
Feeling humbled and beautiful,
Raise up the demands!

I can take your challenge now.
Not sure how,

But finally I believe
In myself.

Wow.

One Way Through

Want me for my body?
Forget it.
Want me for this mind?
Cool.

Want me for my soul?
Now we're talking.

Want to hear this secret?
Whisper into me.

Beyond the bridge,
Everything is different.

All the smart minds are confused,
And the simple souls are laughing.

There is only one way through this suffering,

Bowing lower and lower,
Forever and ever,
Amen.

Love like Water

My eyes are wet with tears
For the years we have been killing.

For the fears we have been tilling-
Fertile soil for fighting
In this culture of hate.

Drawing lines of colors, creeds, and misdeeds
Like we are not awake.

But brother *I am!*
And all I can whisper in this tender state
Is *Amen.*

I am praying-
Not to some false god,
But to the stretching sky!

To the invisible intelligence
That shouts with every cell in my body,
We are so alive!

My humanity is asking,
Who decided to keep killing?
I guess with bills and votes and signatures
Away it is given.

Peace from within is the mainstay-
From here is how we deal with our dearest.

Next is the way we treat people passing on the street.
Lastly the *'far away'*.

I am not asking for any allegiance
But to the united human beings,

The one race that is here on the face
Of this spinning wonder.

If we truly held hands beyond the belief system lands,
We could be laughing,
Ending poverty.

So meet me at the borders and gates,
The places where we need love like water,
Crate by crate.

It's never too late
To keep
Giving.

Kiss You On the Lips

I write poetry
To believe in
What I hope for.

I am just grasping at words
And meanings,

Hoping, praying,
Waiting, saying,

"Is this love?
Is this it?"

This poetry wants
To kiss you on the lips.

Hidden Within

I know two women
Who live down the street.

One tromps in the material,
-The other *immaterial,*
Set free.

The lady who sees without seeing
Asks about my eyes and feeling.
She's undiminished in this hazy light.

While the material girl
Swallows herself whole
And leaves nothing left for me
To unite with.

But wait, you say,
That cannot be,
Something must be left.

Oh good, oh good.
Come closer then,

Let's wrap our
Minds together,

Let's breathe
Into each other's skin,

And reveal
What's hidden within.

Love Me Past This Pain

Hey I've been dying since I was born.
Crying out, this body needs a new home.
Mother wrapped me in her arms saying *welcome* from her womb.
Now I'm 32, headed someday for the tomb.

With a string of sins and rounds of love still echoing through me,
My body decaying but something else lives on.
Had to put it in a song with these words saying love on.

My body is a vessel that I'll leave on the shore,
But this mind is the surface of my heart that will soar.
And I don't mean through the sky,
I mean through the truth that you and I
Are sacred and everlasting.

But these bodies happening fade.
And we're trying so hard to hold on to them, hey?
Click, click, take another pic,
Let's see those curves like never before,
I'm crying out for more!

Somebody love me past this pain!
How else could dying
Birth me again?

People distracting from the pain like take a hit off of these!
Breathe real deep, soon you'll be numb to the beat.
Which makes it easier to go down.
I can maybe even get up and move around,
Forgetting what I came here to remember.

Which is buried beneath the ocean of our pain,
A silent treasure that rises to the surface.

Yes, I mean the essence of love, peace, and mercy,

Crying out from the prophets and lovers and saints,
From the sinners that made amends and said amen,
God is great!

I bow down to a greater force that is the true north,
Because everywhere else is falling off the map. I didn't draw it flat
But the mind can only grasp two sides of the globe
When really it's a spectrum of light- around we go.

And where are you headed tonight with your light?
We can go down and in and close our eyes
To feel what's inside, and then we come up and out
Anchored to a deeper wellspring, alive!

Knowing that love is real and
We can feel this pain newly again.

Let it rain again, I'm crying tears and tears
For the years and years of running away, forgetting about my
Beautiful destiny with a beautiful pain.

And here I am with fancy words and hollow chords that show- what?
My body could be a beautiful thing,
But this life ain't a picture, it's a running stream!

I never thought that I was mean, but I turned away.
How can I turn back? I sit in the quiet and pray,
And then I get up and live a beautiful life, ay?

How can you measure its worth because I see rat race runners
Racking up points and zeroes like they're modern heroes.
So what you're a millionaire?
How much time do you have to connect with what you love?
I'm talking about breathing in the pure air

With your brothers, sisters, and friends?
Lovers and beloveds, deeper and deeper again.
Human connection is what we need,

Yet as we breathe, we don't even know how,
Because this society is living on the surface of material clout,
And we're going insane.

Are you going to believe that karma doesn't happen?
It's hard to believe that all the scientists are laughing
At our inevitable return to the source.

People have understood this since the beginning of time,
Yet we're at the peak of ignorance of what's yours and mine.
We're taking and taking resources and lives
Like the American Empire strikes back!

But we live in a circle,
And that karma's coming back!

So I'm on my knees, begging you please,
To forgive some of your pain.
I know it's weighing heavy,
Pushing you down again.

I'm sorry for my mistakes and doubt.
I don't even know you, so how can it work out?
How can you trust with bust after bust,
And you're reeling from the scars?

I can't see in the dark,
But the sun comes up in an infinite arc
Towards the One,

And there's a light inside of me
Singing we are one!

III. DISCOVERING AN OASIS

A Secret Door

I found a secret door
Into a garden,

But then it turned
To flames!

Now it's ashes,
And I'm covering my skin,
Wondering

What will be born
Again?

The Sweetness of Your Longing

All this waiting,
When will it end?

It feels like we're just standing around,
Hoping for some savior.

Rise up my brother,
Sister, friend,

Now is the time
For us to seize our love again.

Diving into the sea
Of love's unity.

Are these just mere words?
These are signs,

Look, breathe,
Stretch, open.
Nourish with food
And drink and friends.

Laughter and tears,
Floating and delving into
Depths.

Have you tasted
The sweetness
Of your longing?

Pearls pass
Many moons,

Then one day,
Perfected.

Here we are,
Open your shell,

Reveal the splendor
Of your skin

And we're off flying!

Breathe into Your Body

Breathe into your body.

When you can breathe into
Every part,

Breathe into her.

When you can breathe into
Every part of her,

You'll be One.

So Full of Love

I am so full of love,

I am a heretic,
Casting doubts
In the minds
Of reasoning men.

I am so full of love,

I am drunk on the sound
Of your laughter,
The sound of your heart
Singing.

I am so full of love,

I am a fool,
Intoxicated with the possibility
Of true love and the evolution
Of the human spirit.

I am so full of love,

I can barely speak,
I can barely hold up a sign
That points to the truth,

Which is that we have
Oh so many heavily guarded notions
Which are simply untrue.

Who am I to criticize?
I am in many ways failing.

But the love in me
Keeps pushing everything I am
Off a cliff,

Everything except
The bare essentials of
Body and skin,
Mind and heart,

And an infinite ideal of love
Being the only thing
That is real!

I am so full of love!

Do you remember your joy?
Your youthful fascination
With the absolutely stunning
Revelations of nature?

Are you in-touch
With your body's choir
Of vocal chords
And orgasmic worlds
That lie quietly latent?

Volcanoes and the coming spring
Have nothing on the universe of making love
And the way you would sing!

When those waves that you aroused
Reached their peak and crashed down,
Dissolving into the sea
Of love's unity.

I am so full of love,

That no drug, no heady words, no procession,
Could fully give service
To the realization
That everything lives for love.

Which means there is no-thing to do,
Just every-thing to be,
So full of love.

I am so full of love,

That I am begging you
To be too,

To return
To what your heart longs for most,
And leave the world
Of reasonable men behind.

Now is the time
For the *lovelution*
To begin its rhyme,
One step at a time,
Until it reaches every doorstep.

Behold,
We are one humanity,
Behold,
Let us live out that simple truth,

And wash in the waves
Of the sun and love's play,

Until healing takes root
In every single heart,
Every single day.

The Moon Ties Us Together

When you can start to feel
The moon bending time and space,

Suddenly your body may realize
That it's made of spiraling stars
Whirling into form!

You are the sun,
You are the moon,
You are these billions of planets rotating.

Circling round and round
In your veins
And eyes and muscles and skin.

Ah, yes,
Your skin…

Wraps universes around me

And *ties us*
Together.

Falling into You

I'm falling down,
I'm falling in,
To You.

One village or
None?

Brother pick up an instrument,
Put down the gun.

Singing
"We are one!"
"We are one!"

Sparking the heat
Of love returning.
Of *love*.

Singing
"We are one!"
"We are one!"

Healing sounds,
Healing breath,
All in one.

Each color
Of the Sun.

Calling Out

Look,
Do you ever imagine
The life of the birds,
Living in the trees,
Calling out?

Calling out to me,
Calling out to you,
Calling out to love?

I heard them singing.

They called me outside,
And I began to hear

A different song,
Something sweeter.

What a Feeling

So in love with you,
What can I do?
Every single day,
Every single night.

I've got this feeling,
Feeling more than alright!
Take me through the night.
You're so bright, so light.

What a feeling!
I can't hide it.
What a feeling!
Deep inside.

So in love with you,
What can I do?

A Shining Star

I was cursing through the night.

Couldn't sleep,
Couldn't eat.

Just separation
From You.

Sleepless,
Breaking down,
At the end of all of this,

Light breaks through.
Who am I now?

Before
I had plans.

Now
I am no-thing
From a shining star.

Before
I was keeping tally-
This side vs. that.

Now
I can't even keep the score.

All I want to do
Is fall

Into
The fountain
Of life.

Heart Says

Mind says
I took a coarse ruby
And polished it into a diamond.

Heart says
I loved deeply.

Soul says
I knew it all along.

Love Knows Your Name

Love knows your name,
Keeps writing to you
Everyday
Since before you were born.

Have you opened
Up the letters?

The pain of life
Is loud, getting louder-

I can barely hear
The quiet peace
Enveloping all of nature.

Until-
Until this very moment,
Where I realize that

Love
Knows my name.

One in Everything

Tonight
The sky was clear,
I could see some stars.

I thought,
Who am I?

And
Who even has the time
For these thoughts anymore?

Not I
Says the politician,
Lying to my face.

Not I
Says the sportsman,
Consumed by race after race.

Not I
Says the scientist,
Always testing and testing.

Aye, Aye
Says the lover!
Resting and resting.

In this one taste,
Remembering to see
One in everything.

Whispering Soon

We fell in love
A week ago,
Dear lover.

What a strange and holy gift
To discover newly
How to live,

How to *give,*
And how to *receive.*

My eyes open differently now,
With your heart in mind.

Love refreshes everything,

And takes the sting
Out of our waiting
For so long.

Dear lover,
Know that God
Is waiting for you,

Whispering to you,
*"Soon,
Yes, soon,*

*We will all
Fall in love
Again!"*

I Believe in Alchemy

I believe in
Alchemy.

I believe in
The healing power of *love*,

And I believe in
Contemplating God's *essence*.

I believe
In the holy and
Mischievous match
Of wrestling *pure spirit*
Into *matter!*

Watch these hands,
Watch these words,

Watch this *alchemy*
Brew and brew,
And stew and stew.

And now you,
With your human curves,
Merge with me,
In a clay-shelled body,

And we dissolve
Into heaven free.

Pure Poetry

If you don't believe
In God,

Let's call it
A universal intelligence?

Living inside of
Everything?

Otherwise,
What *would you say?*

Where is it?
Nowhere? Somehow not
Bursting forth with love?

Have you ever tasted
Salt from the sea
Of unity?

Come,
Come to the filling stations.

Rise,
Like pure
Poetry.

Opening Cages

Love,
Spilling from the pages.

Love,
Opening cages and cages.

Love,
Like never before.

Love,
Like crying out for more!

What does it mean
To have wings?

And how does it feel
To now sing?

To swim and to swing
And to fly?

What am I seeing
In your eye?

Consuming me, consuming you,
I might just die
To being separate.

A Mysterious Force

Some believe in nothing,
Others in a mysterious force.

But the Beloved has
Kissed me without lips,
Touched me without hands,
Held me without a heart,

Revealing that in truth,
Love is real.

And there is no reality
But the *indivisible.*

Draw lines all you want.
When you zoom in or out,
What matters?

I am stretching and learning
To see *one in everything.*

One Village

I'm trying to be "professional,"
Show up impeccably
And leave the rest behind.

But sometimes it's challenging
To comb and clean each inch,
Put on layer after layer,
(Don't miss a spot),

When I've been naked in the sun.
I've been busy adventuring
Across the globe to experience
If indeed we are *one village*.

And we *are*.
And we don't need
Any clothes.

We just need to love,
And to take the time
To see our pain
And our own healing!

Because people love you,
I love you,
We *do*.

And it's not because I need you
Or don't need you,
It's just because here *we are*.

Ubuntu.

I am who I am because of who we are.

This is not just philosophy.
Our bones were made
From the same dust and stars,

The same maker,
A living force inside of us!

So yes, I can't help but untuck and unbutton,
To release all that is unessential,

And lay bare,
Lay my heart and body bare,
Upon the cool smooth stones
Embraced by the sunny sky,

At our favorite wellspring
In heaven.

I Am Not for Me

I am not for me,
But for I.

Who is I?

I is the origin
Of being.

Who is that?

Well who could say?

Travel there inside
And the words go away.

Feel!
With every ounce
Of your being,

The goodness
And grace
Of being
Human.

The Garden of Lovers

I love you like the sun
Longs to kiss the face
Of everything it illuminates.

I love you as
The crowded village streets-
We keep bumping into each other
And I like it.

I love you like
The trees hungry for rain,
Silently awaiting the day
Of resurrection.

Love plants a seed
And grows in need,
And the wisdom pours
From its new leaves.

Taste the fruit
Of all this meaning,

Prepare yourself
To enter the garden of lovers
And never leave.

Axis of the World

On a rocket ship we are climbing.
Borrowed clothes and fuel, time declining.
Where is this going? Ask the curious ones.

Deeper in space is a place
Where nothing gives birth to everything at a timeless pace.
I close my eyes and feel the power.
I turn in these senses and lose the hour.

Inside of this clay shell is a well that never runs dry.
But how can I be so sure,
Except that the prophets say it's true from on high?
I touched that place, but it could have been an illusion.
I shook hands with a messenger,
But someone could've been deluded.

Therefore, I follow the only compass that's mine-
This invitation revealing that *God is real*, take your time.
So I breathe, relax, count my blessings, ready my sacks,
For a great journey into the unknown.

All this pain of the past, and love that didn't last, will be with me.
All my shame and uncertainty, I greet peacefully.

Today I heard an angel after I was praying in the church,
She came from a rainbow gathering
In the mountains up north.

For a moment, I thought God was opening.
In the Venice streets, Heaven disrobing.

Between the cracks of the cobbled concrete,
Light breaking through,
Axis of the world tilting.

Share It with Everyone

I took you in,
You took me in,
We loved it there.

One day we parted ways
With a secret that would stay
Until today.

Here we are now again,
Mirrors,
Looking for each other.

Gaze into *this*,
The eyes of everything.

See the love brimming
And fill your cup.

Share it with everyone.

God's Loving Imagination

I want to meet you
In God's loving
　Imagination.

Oh my heart!

I breathe in,
Exhaling loudly.

My body wakes up!

It begins to move,
Begins to dance,
Begins to let go

Of everything less
Than God's loving
　Imagination.

A Golden Wind

Your beautiful body
Doesn't mean much of anything.

Your willingness to love
Means everything.

Yes, I want your body,
But more, I want your soul's living
Inside of it,
A golden wind in a clay shell.

Nothing else will do,
We are radiance unfolding
Or else our sex will fade...

We are constantly
Being born and dying to what we know,
What we feel, what we see,

What we realize
Sets us free.

IV. COMING HOME

At the Gates

When God
Meets us at the gates,

I pray that
We'll be laughing.

He'll be asking
How everyone felt

Smelling
The Rose?

~

He'll be asking,
Did you share
All that you could?

"Sorry,
I'm sorry...

I could've
Uncorked
More and more
Blessings!"

In A Melting Pot

Naked we are
In a melting pot,

Boiling off our
Lower desires.

As we begin to burn,
The bubbles rise.

People expect
Some kind of revolution,

But I say,
Take off your clothes.

See what it is like to sit in bed
With your eyes closed and your hands

Resting on the cool comfort
Of your own skin.

On The Sea Floor Waiting

Can you celebrate
That someone loves you?

Celebrate
Your right to be here,
And live in love?

Even an animal,
A precious dog,
Is quietly wagging its tail,

Waiting for you
To come home.

Even if you have no one,
Life is there, life is here,
With open hands,
Waiting.

In the eyes of a stranger,
In the sound of a storm,
In a feeling at the deepest depths of despair-

A treasure chest
On the seafloor
Waiting.

Love Languages

Beauty asked me,
How many languages
Do you speak?

I said none
Worth uttering
But the *sound of love*.

All the others are bridges to
Getting there.

You can tell by
Looking into my eyes
How far we've come.

Turn to Prayer

May any thought

You ever have

Turn to prayer.

All The Way Down

Way down,
Outside of the city,
I lost my way
Back home.

Wandering around,
I found the ocean,
You could say
I was reborn.

Hallelujah!

Now I'm going
All the way
Back home.

Spring time!
Love is on my mind!

Where have you been
All this time?

I was busy
Chasing little me!

All the way
Back home.

But now
Something has grown!

Way down,
In the heart of the city,
Finally known!

Mary Oliver

I found Mary
Oliver in the woods,

She was tending carefully
To the present moment

Of squirrels and birds
Making life next to each other.

Their brown hair and perfectly made shapes
Living on as though through a silent pact,

Scrambling across the branches, flying in the air,
Moving on and on with total attention,

Inside this great something
Of wildness.

Be Good to Me

All the way down,
We're going.
All the way up,
We'll be floating.

With the sun in my eyes,
Thinking of you.
With love in my mind,
dreaming of you.

Be good to me,
I'll tell you all my secrets,
I'll take care of you.

All the way down,
Love's forgiving.
All the way up,
Love's lifting!

Tasting this pain,
Salty ocean.
Tasting this love,
I'm diving in!

Be good to me,
I'll be good to you,
I'll take care of you.

My Epitaph

I could die any day.
So could you,
It's true.

What would your epitaph say?

Hopefully mine may read:

"He loved deeply,
Inviting everyone to
Shine all of their colors!
We are united as one
And we need your love!"

Written from me to you,
It's true.

Connecting Me to You

I only want to be
Birthing goodness.

I only want to be
Holding your hand
In the cool summer grass.

We only ever wanted that.

We only ever wanted to
Remember the roots
Of these veins,

Yes, blood traveling,
Our bodies electric,
Moving secret messages down the wire.

Moving faster and faster,
Connecting us,

Connecting
Me to you.

All I Can Remember

Poetry comes
From an inside place.

A silent retreat that
Marinates in the mind.

At the end
Words burst forth,
Line after line.

All I can remember now is
Thank you.

My Eyes Are Spies

My eyes
Are spies

For the One
That resides
In everything.

My heart is a field,
Cultivating miles and miles of yield,

And my feet are running
As fast as they can
Towards You.

Beauty Comes to Me

No need to seek anymore,
Beauty comes to me.

No need to ask anymore,
Beauty explains to me.

She holds my hand,
Takes me in,

Oh,
There is nothing left of me!

Only awe
And beauty making.

Fertile Crescent

Your body
Is a fertile crescent.

These curves
We whirl on were

Unfurled long ago,
Before we even had to know

Of the resplendent
Mercy.

Master of Ambiance

I am a master of ambiance.

Close your eyes,
Watch how these scents
And sounds echo on the walls,
With smells of jasmine flowers
Waving in the sunlight.

Listen to the hollow flutes singing notes
Of pain and ecstasy, side by side,
One in one, together.

Open your eyes,
See into your longing.
Touch her, hold her,

Whisper into her
What you've felt for so long
But never told
Anyone...

If Your Prayers Land Close

If your prayers land close,
Feel free to join me.

Arriving as fellow travelers
Simultaneously
At the source.

We may at last, discover together
The secret temple of love
And desire.

It may reach so deep
That the doors within
Appear to be infinite.

In that case,
You may have lost
Your old self

And rediscovered
The Beloved.

The Light of Everything

I am in the deep heart.
Here language is different.
Here language reveals that we're restrained
By some of our laws.

People are laughing in their homes, saying *we don't follow that.*
But we "pledge allegiance to the flag
Of the United States of America."

My words echo from our freedom,
Yet the world is still hungry,
Crying out, "We need more light and love!"

Which says the old ways of the past have in some ways served us,
But many have got to go.

We really are one human village.
It is time to *end poverty and war.*

One step at a time, loving line by loving rhyme
Which says now, "Here my friend, eat and drink
From these words of cool comfort.

You are inside the deep love, already returning.
Yes, we came from there, long ago."

From this place we reach out, saying I need you,
Saying *I am because we are* this blessed human race.

I saw that place,
I felt what it's like
To be naked in the sun,

Free to exist
As one with everything.

Washing Over Me

All I can feel now is
God washing over me.

Ecstasy when my body slows down enough
To greet the building waves of silence.

Washing over these rocks of grief,
Over and over and over again,

Smoothing them out,
Smoothing me out,
Polishing the mirror.

The Body Calls

The body calls,
The heart answers
This is pure poetry.

How can it go any deeper?

It takes time,
And the waves crashing in.

Here we are,
Swirling in the madness,

Somehow finding priceless peace
In each other's eyes
And the mixing of our bodies.

Presence and touch,
Opening new worlds,
Forever.

Like A Tree

I am like a tree,
Pluck from me!

Take all that I am.
I am nothing,
With so much to give.

Words spilling from the pages,
Music oozing out in all ages.

Body bursting with light,
Taste the fruit of all this meaning.

Oh the tastelessness of life
With no loving.

Modern Mystics

We are modern mystics.
Well, we are nothing.

We are currently the last words
Giving way to silence.

Words which say that
You are one
With everything,
But you are nothing.

God is in everything,
So God is in you,
And so you are everything
And nothing at once.

Which makes you a mystery
Spiraling in space.

Here we are,
Modern mystics,

Rising off the water
Like flames.

Thank you everyone for reading this book!

I welcome your feedback. You can email me at caravanoflovers@gmail.com.

Thank you Denise Roussel for editing this book.

Thank you beautiful poets of the world!

Rumi (*Translations by Coleman Barks and Nader Khalili*), Hafiz (*Translations by Daniel Ladinksy*), Mary Oliver, Pablo Neruda, Anais Nin, Thomas Merton, Billy Collins, Naomi Shihab Nye, Robert Frost, Rupi Kaur, Shel Silverstein, Vanessa Stone, and Dr. Seuss.

Find me at:
Facebook.com/peterjamescraig

Love,
Peter

www.ingramcontent.com/pod-product-compliance
Lightning Source LLC
Chambersburg PA
CBHW032142040426
42449CB00005B/368